The Unchanging Truth

Jesus

Still

The Way, Truth & Life

Dr. David Scott

PCB

Published by Purple Chair Books and Educational Products, LLC
First Printing, 2020
Copyright © Dr. David Scott, 2021 Scott, David 1969-
The Unchanging Truth
Jesus
Still
The Way, Truth & Life
By Dr. David Scott

ISBN: 978-1-953671-01-1

Christian Life/ Spiritual 1.Title
Printed in the United States of America
Set in Adobe Garamond Pro

Interior Designed by Sarco Press

Publisher's Note

THE PURPOSE OF this publication is to offer hope, encouragement, and an alternative worldview from the uncompromised Christian perspective. This book is sold with the understanding that the publisher or author is not engaged in rendering psychological, therapeutic, or other professional services. This product is offered solely for the purpose of education.

Without limiting the rights under copyright reserved above, no part of this publication may be reproduced, stored in or introduced into a retrieval system, or transmitted, in any form, or by any means (electronic, mechanical, photocopying, recording, or otherwise), without the prior written permission of both the copyright owner and the above publisher of this book.

Contents

Dedication vii
Acknowledgment ix
Introduction xi
Chapter One: All Roads Lead to God…Right? 1
Chapter Two: The Bible 7
Chapter Three: Jesus (The LORD's Christ) 13
Chapter Four: Being a Christian 19
Chapter Five: I AM 27
Chapter Six: What's In a Name? 33
Chapter Seven: Salvation and Being Saved 39
Chapter Eight: Jesus (God the Son) 45
Chapter Nine: A Love like No Other 53
Chapter Ten: Hell is a Real Place 61
Final Thoughts 71

Dedication

I DEDICATE THIS book to the men and women throughout the entire world, who continuously without wavering teach, preach and proclaim the gospel of the Lord Jesus Christ. Remain steadfast and determined. I admonish you to hold fast and make your election sure. As laborers in God's Kingdom, remember in love the words of the aged apostle Paul to his young protégé Timothy found in 2 Timothy 4:1-5:

> "I solemnly urge you in the presence of God and Christ Jesus, who will someday judge the living and the dead when he comes to set up his Kingdom: Preach the Word of God. Be prepared, whether or not the time is favorable. Patiently correct, rebuke, and encourage your people with good teaching. For a time is coming when people will no longer listen to sound and wholesome teaching. They will follow their own desires and look for teachers who will tell them whatever their itching ears want to hear. They will reject the truth and chase after myths. But keep a rational mind in every situation. Don't be afraid of suffering for the Lord. Work at telling others the Good News and fully carry out the ministry God has given you."

Acknowledgment

I WOULD LIKE to thank all who encouraged and prayed for me, giving me the strength to accomplish this endeavor. Each of you has greatly impacted my life and destiny. May God continue to bless and prosper you 30, 60, 90, and 1000 fold for your ministry in prayer, and the additional ministries God has entrusted to you. Thank you and God bless and keep you always. Also, I would like to extend the most heartfelt and sincere thank you to my gracious and beautiful First Lady, partner, and companion in the Lord's ministry Tamara DeRamus-Scott. Thank you for standing with me, encouraging me, and supporting me along this journey. TT, you are a treasure!

Introduction

NOW MORE THAN any other time, men and women need the ability to discern the difference between truth, opinions, and men's philosophies. As we witness our society and world spin further and further out of control, there is no time to be skeptical about our immortal souls and where we will spend eternity. We must choose our stand whom or what we will serve and the consequences of that choice. We all must make a choice. Speaking to the children of Israel, the writer said in Joshua 24:14-15, "Fear the Lord and serve him wholeheartedly. Put away forever the idols your ancestors worshiped when they lived beyond the Euphrates River and in Egypt. Serve the Lord alone. But if you refuse to serve the Lord, then choose today whom you will serve." Jesus is the Savior of the world, and not a mere man, teacher, prophet, or sage. He is God, the Son, the second person of the Trinity, and the only door by which we can be saved. The Bible is clear in its declaration that God exists in triune, Father, Son, and Holy Spirit. Jesus is one person of the triune Godhead, God the Father, God the Son, and God the Holy Spirit. Jesus declared this truth by stating, "The Father and I are one."

No other person has been debated, denied, hated, and rejected like Christ. Why? Jesus did not come into this world to cause contentions. He came into the world to save the lost, declaring unapologetically, "I AM the way, the truth, and the life." No other man in history has dared such a bold claim. No other has proven through demonstration and authority that in him and him alone dwells the completeness of God's power. Jesus' life affirmed his claim. He and the Father are one. To Jesus alone is all power delegated in heaven and earth. Jesus alone is the answer to the broken, hurting, struggling, and sin-sick soul. That truth has not changed.

The writer says in John 3:17, "God sent his Son into the world not to judge the world, but to save the world through him." The invitation of salvation is extended to all that call on him. Jesus promises in Matthew 11:28, "Come to me, all of you who are weary and carry heavy burdens, and I will give you rest." That is the unchanging truth!

The Unchanging Truth

Jesus

Still

The Way, Truth &Life

CHAPTER ONE
All Roads Lead to God...Right?

"I AM THE WAY, THE TRUTH, AND THE LIFE: NO MAN COMETH TO THE FATHER BUT BY ME...HE THAT HATH SEEN ME HATH SEEN THE FATHER" JOHN 14: 6, 9.

IN THIS CHANGING world, people routinely develop and adjust their views about everything. Daily, their ideas, opinions, and positions change. In this fast-paced society, for many, there are no absolutes. Everything is relative. Our beliefs, the way we worship, and how we perceive, understand and reach God. The rationale for this way of thinking is simple. It is couched in the belief that everyone has the right create their path, beliefs, and spiritual and religious expression. Because all roads lead to God, right?

The idea, belief that all roads lead to God is correct. It is a fact we will all someday see God regardless of our choices, wrong or right. However, it is more accurate that all choices lead us into the presence of God. Without exception, every man and woman will one day stand in the presence of the living and eternal God. Rich and poor, famous and of no reputation, all will someday appear before his Holy presence. This is an inevitable reality. All creation will behold the majesty of the Designer, Creator, and maker of the Universe. The writer of the book of Revelation called it the Final Judgment of humanity. He said in Revelation 20:11-15:

> "I saw a great white throne and the one sitting on it. The earth and sky fled from his presence, but they found no place to hide. I saw the dead, both great and small, standing before God's throne. And the books were opened, including the Book of Life. And the dead were judged according to what they had done, as recorded in the books. The sea gave up its dead, and death and the grave gave up their dead. And all were judged according to their deeds. Then death and the grave were thrown into the lake of fire. This lake of fire is the second death. And anyone whose name was not found recorded in the Book of Life was thrown into the lake of fire."

Today, those under the age of forty are less religious than any other period. In the United States, religious congregations have been graying for decades. Current trends show young adults are now much less religious than their elders, are far less likely than older generations to identify with a religion, believe in God, or engage in religious practices. According to Pew Research Center, surveys conducted in over 100 countries and territories over the last decade, lower religious observance among younger adults is common worldwide. For whatever reasons, younger people presently are far less religious in terms of organized religion than in the past. As a result, views, ideas, and opinions of those under forty are more personal, individualistic, and less theologically sound.

Those professing to be spiritual conclude it does not matter what or how we worship. According to this view, truth is your own experience. Whatever makes you feel good and right inside can be god and the validity of your worship. This philosophical stance can be no further from the truth. The writer in Proverbs 14:11 says, "There is a path before each person that seems right, but it ends in death." This false and unsubstantiated idea deceives humanity into believing morality, kindness, and benevolence earns brownie points determining where we spend eternity. That is a lie! Balanced scales, good deeds outweighing evil, will not reserve a place in the afterlife. That, too, is a lie! Also, there is no place called purgatory where we can continue the work of penance and reparations for sin. There is no such place. Good deeds or acts of benevolence will never substitute for the redemption found in Christ. The Bible speaks to this course of thinking saying in Isaiah 64:6, "We are all infected and impure with sin. When we display our righteous deeds, they are nothing but filthy rags." Benevolence without Christ is useless. Nothing we do on our own, for our own motives, or to be justified on our own terms will help us.

In the book of Revelation we learn that all humanity will someday stand before the judge (God) and answer for their decisions and actions while alive on the earth. John the Revelator and witness to the impending day says in Revelation 20:12, "And I saw the dead, small and great, standing before God; and the books were opened: and another book was opened, which is the book of life: and the dead were judged, out of those things which were written in the books, according to their works (deeds)" KJV. Judgment for all humanity is impending reality. The critical equation and factor in this scenario is the decision made for Christ. The connection and relationship with Christ is the essential factor regarding where we spend eternity.

It cannot be overstated that God and Satan are not equal in power. Satan is a created angelic being, and Yahweh/YHWH is the Creator of the Universe. Also, God loves humanity. In contrast, Lucifer is the enemy of God's most precious creation, humans. Satan's hatred toward humankind has been raging since before the world began. Though a powerful spiritual being, Satan does not have the power to destroy us. He must enlist our cooperation to achieve his aim. He uses smoke, mirrors, humanity's arrogance, wisdom, logic, and reason. He tricks us into believing we are gods, or at least demigods. His most effective and deceptive trick is convincing humanity that he does not exist. The most dangerous enemy is the one you are not on the lookout for. Satan is not a little man dressed in a red suit with a pitchfork in hand, but he is the Father of lies. He is the most beautiful creature ever created. Being the chief Cherub, he uses every skill, ability, and tactic at his disposal. He is the great deceiver, manipulating and destroying nations. Believing Satan does not exist, many embrace his lie believing that living decent, moral and ethical lives make us okay, because good people go to heaven. However, this is untrue, and carries devastating and eternal consequences.

Satan tricks the world suggesting and offering alternatives to established biblical standards for life. As a result, men and women choose their own paths, with no consideration of biblical instruction. In countless scenarios men and women choose ways that seem right, creating their own personal gods. The Bible has no value or relevance in their lives. Cleverly, Satan reduces the Bible to a book of philosophies, ideas, and moral teachings, nothing to be taken literally. Through deception, he conceals and hides from the world the truth of his character. He distracts from the words found in 1 Peter 5:8, which tells us, "Be sober, be vigilant; because of your adversary the devil (Satan), as a roaring lion goes about, and seeking whom he may devour." Lucifer presents himself an angel of magnificent light, but he is a terrible and relentless enemy seeking to decimate the whole of humanity if it were possible.

Satan deceives men and women into believing it does not matter whom, what, or how we worship. However, there is only one true God. For centuries, men and women have called many things god. It has been a long tradition and practice of humanity to worship those things they do not understand, or elect to attribute some magical power. These so-called gods are nothing more than lifeless, emotionless, inanimate pieces of wood, metal, rock, marble, human-made images, and idols. These objects have mouths but cannot speak, and definitely, they cannot save. Serving these objects rather than the living God is an abomination. The writer in Psalm 135:15 said,

> "The idols of the nations are merely things of silver and gold, shaped by human hands. They have mouths but cannot speak eyes but cannot see. They have ears but cannot hear, and mouths but cannot breathe. And those who make idols are just like them, as are all who trust in them."

We are all obligated to worship only the one true God of heaven. He alone is worthy of praise and adoration for his glorious acts. He has commanded humanity to worship him, placing nothing else above him. Those that disobey will answer for their actions on the great Day of Judgment. All men and women, small and significant, will stand before his throne. All roads chosen, right or wrong lead to his majesty. Speaking as an eye witness about the impending, the writer said in Revelation 20:11-12:

> "I saw a great white throne and the one sitting on it. The earth and sky fled from his presence, but they found no place to hide. I saw the dead, both great and small, standing before God's throne. And the books were opened, including the Book of Life. And the dead were judged according to what they had done, as recorded in the books."

Whether we accept him as LORD, Savior, and master of our life or not, we will all someday see God! We must all decide whether he will be an adoring father or a righteous and unsympathetic judge. We have a choice. To get eternal life, the writer says in Romans 10:9-13:

> "If you openly declare that Jesus is Lord and believe in your heart that God raised him from the dead, you will be saved. For it is by believing in your heart that you are made right with God, and it is by openly declaring your faith that you are saved. As the Scriptures tell us, "Anyone who trusts in him will never be disgraced." Jew and Gentile are the same in this respect. They have the same Lord, who gives generously to all who call on him. Everyone who calls on the name of the LORD will be saved."

When the deeds and motives of men and women are revealed, there will be weeping, wailing, and indescribable terror for those who disobeyed God's commands, preferring personal pleasures, creating and serving their gods. Those who accepted Jesus the LORD's Christ and obeyed him will be rewarded with joy and peace. They will be rewarded for accepting and holding securely to faith in Christ. Whatever the choice, all roads ultimately lead to God. However, our choices will determine if we will be welcomed before his presence or terrified by his appearance and the certainty of his righteous judgment. Whatever the decision, the writer in Romans 14:10 says,

> "Remember, we will all stand before the judgment seat of God. For the Scriptures say, "As surely as I live,' says the LORD, every knee will bend to me, and every tongue will declare allegiance to God."

CHAPTER TWO
The Bible

"All scripture is given by inspiration of God, and is profitable for doctrine, for reproof, for correction, for instruction in righteousness: That the man of God may be perfect, thoroughly furnished unto all good works" 2 Timothy 3: 16-17.

There are mixed thoughts and opinions about a specific book that circulated and endured over centuries. It has been criticized by countless and rejected by thousands more. However, it has also been embraced and celebrated by nations, rulers, Czars, and Emperors. It has been a source of inspiration for untold millions, past and present, giving scores the courage to suffer and even sacrifice their lives. Unlike any other book, it is the Logos—the breathed Word of God.

Some claim the Bible to be a book written by a single man. Others claim it to be a collection and compilation of inspiring parables, stories, anecdotes, and fairytales. Yet, it has proven to be the irrefutable, battle-tested Word of truth. The Bible is the Word of God, spoken to men's hearts, recorded, and divinely preserved through centuries. Napoleon Bonaparte once said, "The Bible is no mere book, but a living being, with a power, which conquers everything that opposes it." It is God's grand attempt to reach humanity, even when he is rejected. Through Scripture, society is offered an opportunity to glimpse God's heart, mind, character, and compassion. Nothing in the universe is comparable. It is God's love letter. The most fantastic romance ever told. On its pages, is revealed God's love toward humanity, penned to paper by flawed and mortal human.

No less than forty-two different authors wrote what we call the Bible over 1600 years. The canonized (Protestant) version of the Bible is comprised of 39 Old Testament and 27 New Testament, 66 books. We do not include the Apocrypha books in the Protestant canon. It is believed they are not inspired like the others. However, being written by perceived holy men, they are considered valuable for history and instruction in Christian manners and life. Often referred to as deuteron-canonical, there are seven books in the Catholic Bible, Baruch, Judith, 1and 2 Maccabees, Sirach, Tobit, and Wisdom, not included in the Protestant version of the Old Testament.

To the Christian believer, the Bible is the inerrant and infallible word of God. It is God's instruction manual to his followers, detailing the standard of living that pleases Him, leading to eternal life. The Bible presents the standards required of all men and women to come close to the true and eternal God. It is the manual for living victorious and triumphant in this present world while offering a glimpse of the splendor to come. God's word brings the Kingdom of God to earth and among men.

The Bible is God's revelation of his Son Jesus, the Messiah, and Christ. From Genesis to Revelation, the Bible unfolds God's salvation plan to the world through Christ Jesus. The Bible's purpose is to present to the world its redeemer. Of this point, the Bible is clear. The scriptures state Jesus is the authentic Savior of the world. He is perfect, accepted, and the provided sacrifice.

Christ is the chosen propitiation for the lost, the gift that takes the repentant sinner's place before the righteous and holy God's Judgment seat.

The Bible makes specific points clear. Jesus is not an angel, Michael, or any other. He existed with God, the Father, from the beginning of all things. Christ is not a created being or the brother of Lucifer (Satan). He is the Creator, the second person of the Trinity (Triune Godhead). He is God, the Son. According to Scripture, Jesus is the physical expression and manifestation of the unseen God. Stated, he (Jesus) is none other than God himself formed in human flesh. He is the incomprehensible God that longed for fellowship with his creation so desperately that he wrapped a part of himself in the flesh and lived among them. The Scripture makes this understandable in John 1:1:

> "In the beginning, the Word already existed. The Word was with God, and the Word was God. He existed at the beginning with God. He came into the very world he created, but the world didn't recognize him. So the Word became human and made his home among us."

The Scriptures explain before the world was or existed, there was the Word that was not only with God but was God himself. The same Word became flesh and lived among humanity. God took on the form of a man and lived on earth to accomplish a divine purpose. His purpose was to restore humanity in fellowship through Christ Jesus, his beloved son, God, the Son; the Word made flesh.

The Bible informs us that only through the shed blood of Jesus (the Lord's Christ) can sin be forgiven. Only through accepting his sacrifice on the cross at Golgotha can sin's penalty be settled. All humanity can be redeemed if they accept Jesus as Lord and Savior, the only salvation source. There is no other. The

Bible states that Adam's sin entered the world, and by one man, the second Adam (Jesus) sin has been canceled once and for all through him.

The Bible is God's Word. There is no other collection, compilation, or composition like it. It is the irrefutable revelation of the Lord's Christ to a defiant and condemned world. The Bible is God's reaching, offering humanity hope and redemption. Other books have the potential to inspire, motivate, and momentarily empower. The Logos has the power to renew, transform, and restore new life. The writer tells us in Hebrews 4:12-13:

> "The Word of God is alive and powerful. It is sharper than the sharpest two-edged sword, cutting between soul and spirit, joint and marrow. It exposes our innermost thoughts and desires. We hide nothing in all creation from God. Everything is naked before his eyes, and he is the one to whom we are accountable."

God's Word searches the hidden secrets of the heart, exposing our thoughts, ideas, and motives. Also, it changes and empowers lives. Speaking to this point, the writer said in 2 Timothy 3:16-17:

> "You have been taught the Holy Scriptures from childhood, and they have given you the wisdom to receive the salvation that comes by trusting in Christ Jesus. All Scripture is inspired by God and is useful to teach us what is true and to make us realize what is wrong in our lives. It corrects us when we are wrong and teaches us to do what is right. God uses it to prepare and equip his people to do every good work."

Being God's breathed word the Bible is infallible in principle. God's word never fails. The promises of God are reliable. Having no respect for a person, all humanity can embrace his word and experience transforming power. Not only does his word speak life into dead situations and circumstances, it unapologetically reveals the source of life, Jesus Christ, the living Word.

CHAPTER THREE
Jesus (The LORD's Christ)

"IN THE BEGINNING WAS THE WORD, AND THE WORD WAS WITH GOD, AND THE WORD WAS GOD. THE SAME WAS AT THE BEGINNING WITH GOD. ALL THINGS WERE MADE BY HIM, AND WITHOUT HIM WAS NOT ANYTHING MADE THAT WAS MADE...AND THE WORD WAS MADE FLESH AND DWELT AMONG US, AND WE BEHELD HIS GLORY, THE GLORY AS OF THE ONLY BEGOTTEN OF THE FATHER, FULL OF GRACE AND TRUTH" JOHN 1:1-3, 14.

THE SCRIPTURES ARE clear about Jesus of Nazareth. He is the one the prophets said would come into the world and save lost men and women from their sins. He was born of a virgin in Bethlehem and called the seed of Jesse and David's offspring. He is the adopted son of the carpenter named Joseph. He is the Savior of the world, God manifested in the flesh, both human and divine. He was crucified on a tree, nailed in his hands, pierced in his side and feet, having have a crown of thorns placed on his head, and hailed King of the Jews. He is called the Prince of Salem and the High Priest after the order of Melchizedek. He is identified in the book of Isaiah as the Suffering Servant. He is the ransom and propitiation for all of humanity's sins. He is called Immanuel, God with us, the Son of Man, and the Son of God.

The scriptures tell us Jesus, born in Bethlehem, was waited for by the prophets, and came into the world fulfilling the words spoken about him from ancient days. Jesus of Nazareth, born of a virgin, is the legitimate Christ, the only begotten Son of the Father. Jesus is the awaited Messiah of the world. He came into the world as a man. However, he was also divine. He was God in the form of flesh (human). He is God, the Son. Jesus is the second person of the Godhead. Scripture is clear and irrefutable concerning this point. According to John 1:

> "In the beginning was the Word (Jesus), and the Word was with God, and the Word (Jesus) was God (not a God). All things were made by him (Jesus), and without him was nothing made that was made. "He was in the world, and the world was made by him, and the world knew him not… The Word (Jesus) was made flesh and dwelt (lived) among us, and we beheld his glory, the glory as of the only begotten of the Father, full of grace and truth."

Though there are many opinions about Jesus, there is only one correct. He is the only hope for a sin-sick, morally depraved, and wickedly corrupt world. He alone can save and redeem. Throughout history there have been scores of teachers, philosophers, self-proclaimed holy men, and prophets, but only one valid Savior. Many have claimed to be of some reputation. Yet, only Christ Jesus, through signs, wonders, and miracle after miracle, fulfilling every prophecy concerning him in Scripture, has proven legitimate. Only Christ has cast out demonic spirits, opened blinded eyes, unstopped deaf ears, caused mute tongues to speak, and fed thousands with whatever placed before him, raised the dead back to life, and became victorious over death and the grave. There is only one Jesus, the LORD's Christ, called a Galilean, the Son of the Highest, the bright and morning star, the

Lion of the tribe of Judah, the head of the church, and the apostle and high priest of our profession, Jesus, the Lord. He alone is the revealed one of scripture, both Lord and Christ.

Every man and woman professing to be Christians must believe what the scriptures declare concerning their Savior. There is no other viable record or account concerning him. The scriptures alone teach us about God and his Christ. Men inspired by the Holy Spirit to make a testament concerning the Savior, wrote what is now the Bible. The scripture's primary purpose is to provide humanity a way to know God, recognize his Christ, and receive him personally as Savior and Lord. Selected men of God have given us his Word as the truth and light in a dark and depraved world.

The Bible tells us Jesus, God the Son, became flesh, to die as a sacrifice for the world's sins. No mere man can take away or forgive sin. Only God can forgive and blot out the stain of sin. God wrapped himself in the form of a man (Jesus) to satisfy the penalty of sin, death. God the Son, laid aside the rights and privileges of deity, made himself a man so he could die and render sin powerless once and for all. He made himself a humble servant with human frailty and weakness, yet he remained sinless and undefiled by the influence of the world. The writer informs us in Hebrews 2:14-18:

> "Because God's children are human beings—made of flesh and blood—the Son also became flesh and blood. For only as a human being could he die, and only by dying could he break the power of the devil who had the power of death. Only in this way could he set free all who have lived their lives as slaves to the fear of dying. We also know that the Son did not come to help angels; he came to help the descendants of Abraham. Therefore, he needed to be made in every respect like us, his brothers, and sisters so

he could be our merciful and faithful High Priest before God. Then he could offer a sacrifice that would take away the sins of the people. Since he has gone through suffering and testing, he can help us when we are being tested."

The book of Philippians speaks of Jesus' humility and shows us his perfect example while also expressing his deity. The writer of Philippians 2:6-8 says,

"Though he was God, he did not think of equality with God as something to cling to.

> Instead, he gave up his divine privileges; he took the humble position of a slave and was born as a human being. When he appeared in human form, he humbled himself in obedience to God and died a criminal's death on a cross."

About Jesus, the apostle Paul, the great evangelist to the world, said in Colossians 1:15-20:

> "Christ is the visible image of the invisible God. He existed before anything was created and is supreme over all creation, for through him, God created everything in the heavenly realms and on earth. He made the things we can see and the things we can't see—such as thrones, kingdoms, rulers, and authorities in the unseen world. Everything was created through him and for him. He existed before anything else, and he holds all creation together. Christ is also the head of the church, which is his body. He is the beginning, supreme over all who rise from the dead. So he is first in everything. For God in all his fullness was pleased to live in Christ, and through him, God reconciled everything to himself. He made peace

with everything in heaven and on earth by Christ's blood on the cross."

On this matter, the writer of 1John 2:21-23 says,

"I am writing to you not because you don't know the truth, but because you know the difference between truth and lies. Who is a liar? Anyone who says that Jesus is not the Christ. Anyone who denies the Father and the Son is an antichrist. Anyone who denies the Son doesn't have the Father, either. But anyone who acknowledges the Son has the Father also."

CHAPTER FOUR
Being a Christian

"Verily, verily, I say unto thee, except a man is born of water and of the Spirit, he cannot enter the Kingdom of God. That which is born of the flesh is flesh, and that which is born of the Spirit is spirit. Ye must be born (from above) again," John 3:5-6, 7.

What does it mean to be a Christian? Today, there are scores of people who call themselves Christians yet do not understand what it means. The world is quite liberal and broad, with views of what makes one a Christian and Christianity. Many have created unique and self-serving ideas, opinions, and definitions of a Christian. However, no one has the right or privilege to choose ideas and opinions about being a Christian. The Bible gives us a clear, concrete, and well-defined perspective of what it means to be a Christian. Historically, to be a Christian meant to be a follower, imitator, and close copy of the Lord Jesus Christ. Being a Christian has always meant to be like Christ. Through demonstration, Christ himself provided the example we should follow.

Let us begin by stating the obvious. No one can be born a Christian. We are not Christians because we attend church services or perform acts of kindness, charity, or benevolence. Also, we are not Christians because we give sizeable donations to churches, denominations, or religious organizations. Despite popular belief, we can no more call ourselves Christians for any of these reasons than call ourselves cars or automobiles because we spend significant time in the garage. To be a Christian, we must commit to being followers of Christ. We must accept Jesus Christ as both Lord and Savior and do the will of God. Only then are we Christians. Even after deciding to follow Christ, we must continue in our obedience to him. We cannot choose our definition. The writer said in John 8:31, "Jesus said to the people who believed in him, "You are truly my disciples if you remain faithful to my teachings."

It has become vogue and advantages in some circles and communities to profess to be a Christian. Historically, identifying as a Christian was a badge of dishonor and, for many, a death sentence. Those who identified as Christians did so understanding the consequences of that profession. They gave the name Christian to a distinct, peculiar, and committed group of followers of Jesus. Only the committed to Christ can rightfully call themselves Christians. Believers were called Christians at Antioch because of their behavior, attitude, and character, even amid adversity and persecution. His followers emulated him so closely that those around them knew they were his disciples. The moniker Christians was meant to be a slander because they were so Christ-like. As his followers and children, we should be like him. The scriptures tell us in Acts 11:25-26:

> "Then Barnabas went on to Tarsus to look for Saul. When he found him, he brought him back to Antioch. Both of them stayed there with the church for a full year, teaching large crowds of people. It was at Antioch that the believers were first called Christians."

The Unchanging Truth

To be a Christian, faith in Jesus alone is essential. We must acknowledge Christ as the only Savior of the world. He alone must be regarded as the only way to salvation, and the only atonement for the complete work of redemption. Jesus made clear the identifying mark of his disciples, saying in John 13:34-35, "Love each other. Just as I have loved you, love each other. Your love for one another will prove to the world that you are my disciples." By implication, Christians should be committed to serving each other selflessly, even at a personal sacrifice. To say that we are Christian's and do not, cannot, and will not love other brothers and sisters in the faith makes us liars. Not only are we not Christians, we do not know God or genuinely have his spirit. It does not matter if they are not part of our specific denominations, worship as we do, or practice exactly as we do. Jesus had to correct his disciples in the past surrounding the wrong idea. The scripture says in Mark 9:38-40:

> John said to Jesus, "Teacher, we saw someone using your name to cast out demons, but we told him to stop because he wasn't in our group." "Don't stop him!" Jesus said. "No one who performs a miracle in my name will soon be able to speak evil of me. Anyone who is not against us is for us.

Unconditional love for brothers and sisters in the faith is the true mark of a Christian, a follower, and an emulator of the Lord Jesus. The Lord says in John 14:21, "Those who accept my commandments and obey them are the ones who love me. And because they love me, my Father will love them. And I will love them and reveal myself to each of them."

Jesus promised loyal followers they would have his Spirit, character, and manifested nature abiding inside them. Christians have the promise of God's power living in them, leading, and guiding, showing the love Jesus showed. Only Christians have the hope and assurance of receiving the Spirit of God. The writer says in Romans 8:9, 14: "If any man has not the spirit of Christ, he is none of his… For as many as are led by the spirit of God, they are the sons of God." If we do not have God's spirit, we are not his children, and he is not our Father. Either voluntarily or involuntarily, we are in darkness. To be children of God and walking in the light, we must intentionally choose, follow, and emulate Christ. No one becomes a Christian and follower of the Lord Jesus by accident. It is always a sober decision. It is always through deliberation. The Scriptures tell us to count the cost and then decide. We can ask God for his spirit. He is a loving and generous father. The writer records the words of the Lord Jesus in Luke 11:11-13:

> "If your children ask for a fish, do you give them a snake instead? Or if they ask for an egg, do you give them a scorpion? Of course not! So if you sinful people know how to give good gifts to your children, how much more will your heavenly Father give the Holy Spirit to those who ask him."

There is only one way to become a Christian and get eternal life. We must commit to serve and follow Christ. We must genuinely accept Christ as Lord and Savior and no other. The writer says in Romans 10:9-13:

> "If you openly declare that Jesus is Lord and believe in your heart that God raised him from the dead, you will be saved. For it is by believing in your heart that you are made right with God, and it is by openly declaring your faith that you are saved. As the Scriptures tell us, "Anyone who trusts in him will never be disgraced." Jew and Gentile are the same in this respect. They have the same Lord, who

gives generously to all who call on him. "Everyone who calls on the name of the Lord will be saved."

Loyal followers of Christ realize no work or good deed means anything without Christ as Lord and Savior. Every good deed, kind, and benevolent act means nothing outside the relationship and fellowship of Christ. We cannot do enough good, earn enough brownie points, do enough charity, or give enough alms to earn a place in heaven. Every man and woman must accept the free and precious gift of salvation offered by God through his Christ, the Lord Jesus. The writer says in Galatians 2:16:

"We know that a person is made right with God by faith in Jesus Christ, not by obeying the law. And we have believed in Christ Jesus so that we might be made right with God because of our faith in Christ, not because we have obeyed the law. For no one will ever be made right with God by obeying the law."

The scriptures admonish us not to deceive ourselves. Christians walk in the Spirit of God, and only children of God have his Spirit. Jesus must be our only Lord and Savior. The writer says in John 1:12-13, "To all who believed him and accepted him, he gave the right to become children of God. They are reborn—not with a physical birth resulting from human passion or plan, but a birth that comes from God." As children of God, we have become new creatures. The old nature and passions have passed away. We are no longer slaves to our desires and imaginations. The power to overcome now lives in us. Greater is he that lives inside us, than he that lives and rules the carnal world. As children of God, we have the Spirit and nature of Christ in place of the old sinful nature. We have become light and were once in darkness. Unlike those that say they are Christians and are not, the scriptures tell us to walk in the Spirit of God that we may not do the things we once did in ignorance. It tells us in Galatians 5:16-24:

> "Let the Holy Spirit guide your lives. Then you won't be doing what your sinful nature craves. The sinful nature wants to do evil, which is just the opposite of what the Spirit wants. And the Spirit gives us desires that are the opposite of what the sinful nature desires. These two forces are always fighting each other, so you are not free to carry out your good intentions. When you follow the desires of your sinful nature, the results are apparent: sexual immorality, impurity, lustful pleasures, idolatry, sorcery, hostility, quarreling, jealousy, outbursts of anger, selfish ambition, dissension, division, envy, drunkenness, wild parties, and other sins like these. Let me tell you again, as I have before, that anyone living that life will not inherit the Kingdom of God.
>
> But the Holy Spirit produces this kind of fruit in our lives: love, joy, peace, patience, kindness, goodness, faithfulness, gentleness, and self-control. There is no law against these things! Those who belong to Christ Jesus have nailed their sinful passions and desires to his cross and crucified them there. Since we are living by the Spirit, let us follow the Spirit's leading in every part of our lives."

It is hard for many of us to imagine that being kind, good, moral, ethical, and charitable will never earn us a place closer to heaven. However, this is the irrefutable truth. Heaven is a place for a prepared people. No one will get there by mistake. To follow Christ demands a clear, sober, and conscientious decision. Jesus is the stairway and the narrow door by which all must enter. In Matthew 1:3, 6, Jesus says to his disciples,

The Unchanging Truth

"Don't let your hearts be troubled. Trust in God and trust also in me. There is more than enough room in my Father's home. If this were not so, would I have told you that I am going to prepare a place for you? When everything is ready, I will come and get you, so you will always be with me where I am…"I am the way, the truth, and the life. No one can come to the Father except through me."

As followers of Christ, and children of the living God, Titus 2:12-14 reminds us,

"We are instructed to turn from godless living and sinful pleasures. We should live in this evil world with wisdom, righteousness, and devotion to God, while we look forward with hope to that wonderful day when the glory of our great God and Savior, Jesus Christ, will be revealed. He gave his life to free us from every kind of sin, to cleanse us, and to make us his very own people, totally committed to doing good deeds."

CHAPTER FIVE

I AM

"There is one God, and one mediator between God and men, the man Christ Jesus; Who gave himself a ransom for all..." 1 Timothy 2:5-6.

Jesus is the greatest teacher to ever live. History affirms he possessed an effective way of painting pictures for his audiences using images, expressions, phrases, and practical situations he knew they could relate. He often used parables and stories to express and convey the truth about himself and the Kingdom of God. Though brilliant, his listeners often failed to understand and often misinterpreted his words and correct meaning. Not unlike the present, the eyes of many were blinded to the truth. The scriptures tell us in John 12:40 even the prophets long ago said,

> "The Lord has blinded their eyes and hardened their hearts—so that their eyes cannot see, and their hearts cannot understand, and they cannot turn to me and have me heal them." Isaiah was referring to Jesus when he said this because he saw the future and spoke of the Messiah's glory."

Jesus made statements that continue to reverberate through time. However, his words are eternally right. Christ's words are liberating. Jesus is the fullness of hope to all seeking escape from the wrath awaiting a disobedient, unbelieving, unrepentant, and Christ-rejecting world. Centuries ago, Jesus made a promise expected by his followers until this very hour. Offering comfort, Jesus said in John 14:1-3:

> "Don't let your hearts be troubled. Trust in God, and trust also in me. There is more than enough room in my Father's home. If this were not so, would I have told you I am going to prepare a place for you? When everything is ready, I will come and get you, so you will always be with me where I am."

As his children, we often cannot comprehend the words of our Lord and Master. However, he is always willing to remind us, strengthen us, and reaffirm the truth with even greater clarity. It shows this when the disciple Thomas was not afraid to reveal his heart. Thomas expressed what he and the other disciples felt. They did not understand. Thomas said, "No, we don't know, Lord," "We have no idea where you are going, so how can we know the way?" Stated, Thomas confessed he did not know where Jesus was going or how to follow. In response, Jesus made the most profound statement the world has ever heard. Understanding Thomas' and the other disciple's confusion, Jesus clarified his meaning, saying, "I AM the way, the truth, and the life. No one can come to the Father except through me." These words remain true and forever immutable.

The words in John 14:6 imply Jesus alone is the narrow way, the single door to the physical presence of God. In his words, Jesus confirms there is no alternative. He is the only path, and few find "The Way" because of their unwillingness to accept him.

However, Jesus assures salvation and eternal life to all who accept and embrace him as savior. Saying IAM the way, he stated he alone is the way to genuine peace. Asserting I AM the TRUTH, Jesus pronounced he is the truth, and his words are reliable. Peter understood this revelation. When Jesus asked his disciples if they would leave him as many others had, Simon Peter's responded, according to John 6:68, "Lord to whom would we go? You alone have the words that give eternal life. We believe them, and we know you are the Holy One of God."

When Jesus proclaimed IAM the LIFE, he announced he alone is the stairway and door that leads to eternal life. He proclaimed boldly he alone can offer life beyond this earthly realm. Stating he is the LIFE, Jesus reminded his followers they will never die, and live eternally in his kingdom. Though the physical body will one day fall asleep, we will live again. He is the resurrection. His declaration IAM the WAY, the Truth, and the Life stands an enduring reminder Jesus is the source of eternal hope, salvation and redemption. He is the resurrection, and our mediation, securing our reconciliation with the living God. The writer says in Hebrews 4:14-16:

> "So then, since we have a great High Priest who has entered heaven, Jesus the Son of God, let us hold firmly to what we believe. This High Priest of ours understands our weaknesses, for he faced all of the same testings we do, yet he did not sin. So let us come boldly to the throne of our gracious God. There we will receive his mercy, and we will find grace to help us when we need it most."

The scriptures are clear; all men and women born share the penalty of their common ancestor, Adam. Because of Adam's disobedience, humankind inherited the curse of sin. Because of sin, no man or woman on merit alone can be right with God unless the price for sin is paid. The Scripture says in Romans 3:23, "All have sinned, and fallen short of the glory (perfection) of God." What is the penalty for sin? We are told in Romans 6:23, "The wages of sin is death: but the gift of God is eternal life through Christ Jesus our Lord." Humanity can only be saved and rescued from the judgment of sin by accepting Christ as Lord and Savior. There is no other way or substitute. No belief, practice, ideology, or ritual will satisfy the price that God demands. The Scriptures tell us in Hebrews 10:4-7:

> "It is not possible for the blood of bulls and goats to take away sins. That is why, when Christ came into the world, he said to God, "You did not want animal sacrifices or sin offerings. But you have given me a body to offer. You were not pleased with burnt offerings or other offerings for sin. Then I said, 'Look, I have come to do your will, O God— as is written about me in the Scriptures."

Hope in Christ Jesus is the only way to be made right with God. With his own words, Jesus, the king of glory, declares to humanity an irrefutable and immutable truth, "IAM the way, the truth, and the life." Loving and kind are the characteristics of God. However, he demands a standard of righteousness. Without Christ, no man can meet that standard, yet many reject His gift of redemption and salvation. God has provided a way of escape from impending judgment awaiting an unbelieving world in His kindness. The writer tells us in John 3:16-17:

> "For this is how God loved the world: He gave his one and only Son so that everyone who believes in him will not perish but have eternal life. God sent his Son into the world not to judge the world but to save the world through him. "There is no judgment against anyone who believes in him. But anyone who does not believe in him

The Unchanging Truth

has already been judged for not believing in God's one and only Son."

Only through Christ Jesus is there redemption and forgiveness of sin. Nothing else suffices. Only the priceless, sacrificial blood of Jesus, the Lamb of God, will do. God desires to save, redeem, and restore. He wants none to be lost, separated from Him eternally. Scripture tells us in 2Peter 3:9: "The Lord isn't slow about his promise, as some people think. No, he is patient for your sake. He does not want anyone to be destroyed, but everyone to repent." Many profess to know God, but they know him not. They have a cursory knowledge of him. In Matthew 7:21-23, the Lord says:

> "Not everyone who calls out to me, 'Lord! Lord!' will enter the Kingdom of Heaven. Only those who do the will of my Father in heaven will enter. On judgment day, many will say to me, 'Lord! Lord! We prophesied in your name and cast out demons in your name and performed many miracles in your name.' But I will reply, 'I never knew you. Get away from me, you who break God's laws.'"

In Matthew 15:5-9, the Lord Jesus says:

> "You cancel the Word of God for the sake of your own tradition. You hypocrites! Isaiah was right when he prophesied about you, for he wrote, 'These people honor me with their lips, but their hearts are far from me. Their worship is a farce, for they teach man-made ideas as commands from God.'"

There are many that say they know God, but are deceived. The chaos in their lives is proof they are not near God. The scripture is clear in affirming, where the spirit of the Lord is, there is peace. Disorder is the absence of peace. When the presence of God appears, there is liberation and joy. Wherever light is, darkness has to disperse. God is peace amidst any storm. The writer says in 1John 1:5:

> "God is light, and in him is no darkness at all. If we say that we have fellowship with him (God) and walk-in darkness (after this world's patterns and practices), we lie and do not the truth. If we say that we have no sin, we deceive ourselves, and the truth is not in us. If we confess our sins, he is faithful and just to forgive our sins and cleanse us from all unrighteousness."

Through Christ Jesus, God has promised to accept us and enter a relationship. Desperately he longs for fellowship with us. It has been his great desire since the garden. However, beginning with Adam and Eve, sin separated us from him. Corruption impedes intimacy with God. All men and women sin and fall short of God's standard of perfection. However, Scripture reminds us in 1John 2:1:

> "If any man sins, we have an advocate with the Father, Jesus Christ the righteous: And he is the propitiation (sacrifice) for our sins: and not ours only, but also for the sins of the whole world."

CHAPTER SIX
What's In a Name?

"A good name is rather to be chosen than great riches..." Proverbs 22:1.

"Wherefore God also hath highly exalted him, and given him a name is above every name: That at the name of Jesus every knee should bow, of things in heaven, and things under the earth; And that every tongue should confess that Jesus Christ is Lord, to the glory of God the Father." Philippians 2:9-11.

A name is more than an identifier. It provides descriptions, characteristics, and necessary details. A name distinguishes a thing, individual, or family from another. Since days immemorial, we have taken great care to choose and attribute the right name. It has been long believed that a child's name speaks volumes about purpose, prosperity, and future. We believe the name to reveal much about future and destiny. The great American writer and Lecturer Dale Carnegie said, "Names are the sweetest and most important sound in any language."

Historically, a name played a significant role in the place, right, and privilege of one group or individual over another. Nothing speaks more of an individual than a name. Throughout history, people went to great lengths to choose what the family, community, or clan considered a good name. Unlike today, in times past, beyond being phonetically appealing, a name spoke enormously in terms of desires and expectations for the child's future. The Bible is full of examples of exciting characters that have lived up to their names. Jesus, the LORD's Christ is no different. His name is the most important ever given.

The scriptures give us a memorable example of the significance of choosing a name with the aged couple, Elizabeth and Zacharias. When the time came for Elizabeth to give birth to her boy child, called the Baptist, there was a great commotion surrounding the child's name. As time drew closer, people gathered and demanded to know what name they would give the child. Many were confident the child would be given his father's name, relative, or some historical or military hero of the nation. However, this would not be the case. The angel of the Lord appeared and declared that the child's name should be called John. Shocked, confused, and rightfully humbled, Zacharias informed the crowd that the boy's name would be John. The crowd marveled because there was no one in his family or clan by that name. The LORD's messenger pronounced that the child's name was John, which means YHWH has been gracious and has shown favor. God had indeed shown favor to Elizabeth and Zacharias because they were old, and Elizabeth had been barren until she conceived the boy child. How important a name must be that the angel of the LORD (Gabriel) pronounced this child's name!

About Jesus, the Christ, Scripture makes a profound and historically impacting statement. According to Acts 4:12: "There is salvation in no one else! God has given no other name under heaven by which we must be saved." Salvation is through no other name except the name of Jesus/Yeshua. Only in the power and authority of the name Jesus' can humanity be redeemed and forgiven of their sins. Only in the matchless name of the LORD's Christ, Jesus, demons tremble and submit in obedience. Only in the power and name of Jesus does the lame walk again, cancers are healed, and the dead live again. There is no equal in power. In no other name is the ability to heal, deliver, and set free physically and spiritually. Authority and power is in the name of Jesus and none other.

In recorded history, in no other name, have countless miracles occurred. By no other authority or power has dead returned to life. Other names have been called upon to no avail. Only in the name of Jesus are peace, joy, and comfort found. In Jesus, the Christ, the only son of the living God, is hope, liberation and redemption found. In no other is there satisfaction for our eternal souls. The writer says in Philippians 2:9-11:

> "God elevated him to the place of highest honor and gave him the name above all other names, that at the name of Jesus every knee should bow, in heaven and on earth and under the earth, and every tongue declare that Jesus Christ is Lord, to the glory of God the Father."

About Jesus, the writer in Colossians 2:9, says, "In him dwells the fullness of the Godhead bodily." The writer in Acts 2:38 says, "Repent, and be baptized every one of you in the name of Jesus Christ for the remission of sins, and ye shall receive the gift of the Holy Ghost." The writer in Acts 16:16:18 says,

> "One day, as we were going down to the place of prayer, we met a slave girl who had a spirit that enabled her to tell the future. She earned a lot of money for her masters by telling fortunes. She followed Paul and the rest of us, shouting, "These men are servants of the Most High God, and they tell you how to be saved." This went on day after day until Paul got so exasperated that he turned and said

to the demon within her, "I command you in the name of Jesus Christ to come out of her." And instantly, it left her."

The angel of the Lord appeared to Mary, the mother of Jesus, just as he had Zacharias the father of John pronouncing and declaring the name of the boy child. The scriptures tell us that Mary was a virgin when the angel appeared. The writer says in Luke 1:27-35:

> "God sent the angel Gabriel to Nazareth, a village in Galilee, to a virgin named Mary. She was engaged to be married to a man named Joseph, a descendant of King David. Gabriel appeared to her and said, "Greetings, favored woman! The Lord is with you!" Confused and disturbed, Mary tried to think what the angel could mean. "Don't be afraid, Mary," the angel told her, "for you have found favor with God! You will conceive and give birth to a son, and you will name him Jesus. He will be very great and will be called the Son of the Most High. The Lord God will give him the throne of his ancestor David. And he will reign over Israel forever; his Kingdom will never end!" Mary asked the angel, "But how can this happen? I am a virgin." The angel replied, "The Holy Spirit will come upon you, and the power of the Most High will overshadow you. So the baby to be born will be holy, and he will be called the Son of God."

The writer in Matthew 1:18-23 says this about Jesus:

> "This is how Jesus the Messiah was born. His mother, Mary, was engaged to be married to Joseph. But before the marriage took place, while she was still a virgin, she became pregnant through the power of the Holy Spirit. To whom she was engaged, Joseph was a righteous man

and did not want to disgrace her publicly, so he decided to break the engagement quietly. As he considered this, an angel of the Lord appeared to him in a dream. "Joseph, son of David," the angel said, "do not be afraid to take Mary as your wife. For the child within her was conceived by the Holy Spirit. And she will have a son, and you are to name him Jesus, for he will save his people from their sins." All of this occurred to fulfill the Lord's message through his prophet: "Look! The virgin will conceive a child! She will give birth to a son, and they will call him Immanuel, which means 'God is with us.'"

The angel said to call him Jesus (Yeshua), for he will save his people from their sins. The name Yeshua means (Deliverer, Savior). Jesus is the Savior of his people and the entire world. The writer said in Luke 2:21, "Eight days later, when the baby was circumcised, he was named Jesus/Yeshua, the name given him by the angel even before he was conceived." Prophesying seven hundred years before his birth, the writer records in Isaiah 9:6:

> "A child is born to us; a son is given to us. The government will rest on his shoulders. And he will be called: Wonderful Counselor, Mighty God, Everlasting Father, and Prince of Peace. His government and its peace will never end. He will rule with fairness and justice from the throne of his ancestor David for all eternity."

CHAPTER SEVEN
Salvation and Being Saved

"THE HEART IS DECEITFUL ABOVE ALL THINGS, AND DESPERATELY WICKED: WHO COULD KNOW IT?" JEREMIAH 17:9.

DESPITE THEORIST'S OPINIONS, which affirm humans are innately good, scripture does not agree. According to scripture, mankind is inherently corrupt. At the core, there is nothing good, pure, and unselfish in humanity apart from being filled with God's Holy Spirit. Most of the world's dire conditions result from human-made war, economics, and the nation's agendas and politics. Does anything ever change? The world's problems stem directly from the state and condition of men's hearts. Change a man's heart, and change the course of his actions, passions, and ambitions impacting his life and the lives of those around him. Conflict, greed, and selfish ambitions leading to wars begin in the heart and imagination. Scripture reminds us no man knows his capacity and potential for evil. We read in Jeremiah 17:9, "The human heart is the most deceitful of all things, and desperately wicked. Who knows how bad it is?" The answer to this question is simple, God alone.

Since the fall of humanity in the Garden of Eden, humankind has continued on a downward and godless spiral. Instead of striving to return to God, society has done what is right in its own eyes. Humankind has continued to act in perpetual rebellion against God, its Creator. Men and women have been lovers of themselves more than (God) their Creator. But, since the fall, God reestablished the fellowship once shared between his prized creation and himself. Sin continues to make intimacy with God impossible. God hates sin. The penalty for sin is sacrifice, blood, and death. Not wanting any to die, God became that sacrifice in the form of Christ, satisfying the penalty requirement once and for all. God the Father sacrificed his son Jesus; the Word made flesh to die as the sacrifice in the place of humanity.

The penalty for humanity's sin demanded a perfect sacrifice, so God made himself that sacrifice. He alone is perfect. God the Father prepared himself a body, called it his son (Jesus God the Son), and died on a cross to set humanity free from the curse of sin initiated by the first man, Adam. A perfect man, Adam began the curse of sin, and a perfect man, Jesus destroyed the penalty for sin, nailing it to the cross. God's plan of salvation and redemption from the beginning involved an extreme sacrifice. God, the Son, the second person of the Trinity, became the sacrifice, dying for sin's he did not commit, showing the Father's immeasurable love for humanity. Jesus became the ransom for humanity's sins, dying a criminal's death, though he was blameless and innocent.

Speaking of his divinity and humanity, Jesus called himself the Son of God and the Son of man. God is an eternal spirit, and that spirit conceived Jesus, making him God the Son. It is reasonable he was human and divine, born of a human woman, but created by the Eternal God's Spirit. God wrapped Himself in the flesh (Jesus) to pay the penalty for humanity's sins. Without his sacrifice, all would die and perish. But God sacrificed Jesus. The Word became flesh, the son of the virgin called Mary. In Matthew 1:21-23, we read:

The Unchanging Truth

"And she will have a son, and you are to name him Jesus, for he will save his people from their sins." All of this occurred to fulfill the Lord's message through his prophet: "Look! The virgin will conceive a child! She will give birth to a son, and they will call him Immanuel, which means 'God is with us.'"

Without Christ's sacrifice, humanity was destined for destruction, forced to face the judgment of a righteous God. Society was and is lost, and without hope, but for God's unfailing love. The moment man disobeyed, God offered redemption. Jesus, the second person of the Godhead, became the offering for humanity's sins, securing our pardon. Through his sacrifice, Jesus became the only way of salvation and door to fellowship with God. Relationship with God the Father begins with an acceptance of his son Jesus, God the Son. There is no way to the Father, except through the Son. Jesus confirms he and the Father are united in John 10:30, "My Father and I are one." About Jesus, the writer says in Colossians 1:14:

"We have redemption (been set free from the power of sin) through his blood, even for the forgiveness of sins: (Jesus) Who is the image of the invisible God, the firstborn of every creature: For by him (Jesus) were all things created, that are in heaven, and that are in earth, visible and invisible, whether they be thrones, or dominions, or principalities, or powers: he created all things, and for him: And he is before all things, and by him, all things consist."

The writer says in John 3:17, God has made Jesus the only door to salvation, saying, "God sent not his Son into the world to condemn the world; but that the world through him might be saved." God has not provided, nor does he recognize any other way. Jesus alone can offer and provide salvation. Without

Christ, no man can have a relationship with God because he and the Father are one. All humanity is offered a relationship with the Father through Christ. Jesus died for that purpose. We read in Luke 19: 10, "The Son of man is come to seek and to save that which was lost." Humanity is offered eternal life, yet many refuse the Lord's Christ, choosing to follow paths they create and perceive acceptable. However, the scriptures affirm their ideas are wrong. The writer says in John 3:18-19:

> "There is no judgment against anyone who believes in him. But anyone who does not believe in him has already been judged for not believing in God's one and only Son. And the judgment is based on this fact: God's light came into the world, but people loved the darkness more than the light, for their actions were evil."

The salvation of humankind is contingent on one factor, acceptance of Jesus as a personal Savior. There is no escape from the trappings and penalty of sin by our merit. The only hope for escape and salvation is through Jesus Christ, the living Word of God, and bread of life. Faith in Christ Jesus is the only way the lost can be saved. In a relationship with Christ, we can experience a life of communion, joy, and indescribable peace with God. Through Christ alone, we are placed in the right standing and relationship with God. The writer says in John 6:33-35:

> "The true bread of God is the one who comes down from heaven and gives life to the world."... Jesus replied, "I am the bread of life. Whoever comes to me will never be hungry again. Whoever believes in me will never be thirsty."

The scriptures declare if we put our hope and trust in Jesus the LORD's Christ, we will find satisfaction for the longing, hunger, and thirst in our souls. Jesus is our rest and gives life to the soul. He will make alive those that hope in him. Jesus says in John 5:21, 26:

> "Just as the Father gives life to those he raises from the dead, so the Son gives life to anyone he wants... The Father has life in himself, and he has granted that same life-giving power to his Son."

Religion, spiritual practices, new age beliefs, traditions, or superstitions cannot save. Only faith in Jesus, the LORD's Christ, can save. There is salvation in no other. The writer says in Acts 4:10-12:

> "Let me clearly state to all of you and all the people of Israel that he was healed by the powerful name of Jesus Christ the Nazarene, the man you crucified but whom God raised from the dead. For Jesus is the one referred to in the Scriptures, where it says, 'The stone that you builders rejected has now become the cornerstone. There is salvation in no one else! God has given no other name under heaven by which we must be saved."

Scores of men and women refuse to accept Jesus as the only way to eternal life. In their ignorance, they rely on fables, rituals, philosophies, and men's traditions. Some pray to the Universe, rejecting the Creator of the Universe! Far too many want to be spiritual, yet deny the God and Lord of all spirits. Jesus says in John 5:39-43:

> "You search the Scriptures because you think they give you eternal life. But the Scriptures point to me! Yet you refuse to come to me to receive this life. I know you don't have God's love within you. I have come to you in my Father's

name, and you have rejected me. Yet if others come in their own name, you gladly welcome them. No wonder you can't believe! For you gladly honor each other, but you don't care about the honor that comes from the one who alone is God."

In his words, Jesus confirms, he is the only one who can save, yet men and women refuse him. He proclaims, I have come in the authority of my Father, who is the eternal God, and you will not believe what the scriptures reveal about me. However, another will come with no authority, legitimacy, or equal power, and him you will accept. Jesus, The Bread of Life, longs to satisfy our desires for peace, joy, and life. He says to us in Matthew 11:28-29:

> "Come to me, all of you who are weary and carry heavy burdens, and I will give you rest. Take my yoke upon you. Let me teach you because I am humble and gentle at heart, and you will find rest for your souls. My yoke is easy to bear, and the burden I give you is light."

CHAPTER EIGHT
Jesus (God the Son)

"HE IS THE IMAGE OF THE INVISIBLE GOD, THE FIRSTBORN OF ALL CREATION. FOR BY HIM ALL THINGS WERE CREATED, IN HEAVEN AND ON EARTH, VISIBLE AND INVISIBLE, WHETHER THRONES OR DOMINIONS OR RULERS OR AUTHORITIES—ALL THINGS WERE CREATED THROUGH HIM AND FOR HIM" COLOSSIANS 1:15-16.

Though hard to grasp by some, Jesus is God! Yes, he is the one that came down from heaven, Mary's baby, the Son of man, known as the son of the carpenter Joseph, and also called the Son of God. However, irrefutably, Christ is God the Son, the second person of the Trinity. He was with God the Father since the beginning. The scriptures tell us in Genesis 1:26:

> "Then God said, "Let us make human beings in our image, to be like us. They will reign over the fish in the sea, the birds in the sky, the livestock, all the wild animals on the earth, and the small animals that scurry along the ground." So God created human beings in his image. In the image of God, he created them; male and female, he created them."

When God said, "Let us make human beings in our image, to be like us," he was not as many have wrongly concluded and believed addressing the angelic host. He was speaking to God the Son, the second person of the Trinity. God did not need to talk with anyone about his plan; he is God. God, the Father is the Designer and Creator of the Universe and everything in it. Why would God address created creatures and beings about his intentions? Angels and all other created things except humankind do not have the capacity or ability to create. The Divine Creator would never consult a creature or created thing about creation. However, he would consult an equal Creator, the Triune's second person, God the Son (Jesus).

Angels are not created in the image and likeness of God. They are excellent and superior beings. However, they are not like God. There is not a single scripture or ancient text that leads us to believe angels are like God. They cannot create or design other creatures. Even Lucifer, the greatest Cherubim, was not a Creation participant. His jealously of humanity caused his forced rejection from heaven and his standing among the angelic hosts. Even Gabriel, the great and awe-inspiring "Messenger" that stands in the presence of the Eternal One, is not like God. The Archangel Michael who leads the Lord's army of angels in war, the great prince, cannot create like God. He, too, is only one of the created creatures.

When God the Father says in Genesis 1:26: "Let us make human beings in our image, to be like us," he was speaking to the second person of the Triune, the one who would come to earth and save humanity from their sins, Jesus, his only son. The scriptures tell us in Luke 1:26-35:

> "God sent the angel Gabriel to Nazareth, a village in Galilee, to a virgin named Mary. She was engaged to be married to a man named Joseph, a descendant of King

David. Gabriel appeared to her and said, "Greetings, favored woman! The Lord is with you!" Confused and disturbed, Mary tried to think what the angel could mean. "Don't be afraid, Mary," the angel told her, "for you have found favor with God! You will conceive and give birth to a son, and you will name him Jesus. He will be very great and will be called the Son of the Most High. The Lord God will give him the throne of his ancestor David. And he will reign over Israel forever; his Kingdom will never end!" Mary asked the angel, "But how can this happen? I am a virgin." The angel replied, "The Holy Spirit will come upon you, and the power of the Most High will overshadow you. So the baby to be born will be holy, and he will be called the Son of God."

Jesus is God the Son, joined in unity with God, the Father before the world began. To refute or dismiss this claim demands a high degree of intentional, deliberate, and poor Scripture exegesis. It requires significant effort to reject and deny unambiguous evidence from historical and biblical sources. The disciple and apostle, often referred to as the Disciple that Jesus Loved, tells us Jesus is God the Son, existing in harmony with God the Father before anything existed. The writer says in John 1:1-3:

> "In the beginning, the Word already existed. The Word was with God, and the Word was God. He existed at the beginning with God. God created everything through him, and nothing was created except through him."

John tells us the Word (Logos) already existed with God and was God. He calls the "Word" (He) and says it was God himself. To be clear, Jesus (God the Son) is not a god. He is God (the Son). Providing us with some details about Jesus, he says in John 1:10-18:

"He came into the very world he created, but the world didn't recognize him. He came to his own people, and even they rejected him. But to all who believed him and accepted him, he gave the right to become children of God. They are reborn—not with a physical birth resulting from human passion or plan, but a birth that comes from God."

"So the Word became human and made his home among us. He was full of unfailing love and faithfulness. And we have seen his glory, the glory of the Father's one and only Son. "This is the one I was talking about when I said, 'Someone is coming after me who is far greater than I am, for he existed long before me.'"

"From his abundance, we have all received one gracious blessing after another. For the law was given through Moses, but God's unfailing love and faithfulness came through Jesus Christ. No one has ever seen God (the Father). The unique One who is himself God (the Son) is near to the Father's heart. He has revealed God (Father) to us."

Although there appear to be passages of Scripture that undermine the position Jesus is God the Son, and some attempt to use Jesus' own words to confirm that he is not nor ever claimed to be God, the evidence in text is overwhelming that he is none other than God. Close, deliberate, and fair exegesis of Scripture proves that Jesus not only claimed to be God but is God the Son, the second person of the Triune Godhead. To believe a virgin conceived a child by the Holy Spirit forces us to consider the reality that the child's biological father is God, whose very essence and Spirit are holy. The child conceived and born would be at least part of God and divine. Having one parent human and the

The Unchanging Truth

other Divine, Jesus would be human and divine, both the Son of Man and the Son of God.

There are no less than twenty passages of Scripture that suggest Jesus is God. The Scriptures tell us in John 5:18: "This was why the Jews were seeking all the more to kill him, because not only was he breaking the Sabbath, but he was even calling God his own Father, making himself equal with God." Jesus himself says in John 10:30, "The Father and I are one." The Jews knew well that Jesus claimed to be God by saying that he was, in fact, the Son of God. We know this is true because of what the writer records in John 10:33: "We are not stoning you for any good work, they replied, "but for blasphemy, because you, a mere man, claim to be God."

The writer says in 1 John 5:20: "And we know that the Son of God has come and has given us understanding, so that we may know him who is true; and we are in him who is true, in His Son Jesus Christ. *He is the true God and eternal life.*" Let us also consider the writer's words in John 8:57-58: "The people said, "You aren't even fifty years old. How can you say you have seen Abraham?" Jesus answered, "I tell you the truth, before Abraham was even born, I AM!"

Speaking to the unity of the Father and the Son, Jesus says in John 17:21: "I pray that they will all be one, just as you and I are one—as you are in me, Father, and I am in you. And may they be in us so that the world will believe you sent me." The writer of Philippians 2:5-6 tells the believers in Philippi, "You must have the same attitude that Christ Jesus had. *Though he was God*, he did not think of equality with God as something to cling to." Affirming the divinity of Christ, the writer in Colossians 2:9-10 says, "In him, the whole fullness of deity dwells bodily... He is the head over every power and authority." An initial persecutor of the Church who, for his actions, called himself "The Chief of

Sinners," the apostle Paul says in Romans 9:5, "Abraham, Isaac, and Jacob are their ancestors, and Christ himself was an Israelite as far as his human nature is concerned. And *he is God*, the one who rules over everything and is worthy of eternal praise! Amen."

Though difficult to grasp and understand, doubting does not change the truth. Jesus is God, manifested in the flesh. Scripture reminds us of how Jesus satisfied a disciple's doubt in the past. The scriptures tell us in John 20:24-28:

> "One of the twelve disciples, Thomas (nicknamed the Twin), was not with the others when Jesus came. They told him, "We have seen the Lord!" But he replied, "I won't believe it unless I see the nail wounds in his hands, put my fingers into them, and place my hand into the wound in his side." Eight days later the disciples were together again, and this time Thomas was with them. The doors were locked; but suddenly, as before, Jesus was standing among them. "Peace be with you," he said. Then he said to Thomas, "Put your finger here, and look at my hands. Put your hand into the wound in my side. Don't be faithless any longer. Believe!" Thomas exclaimed "My Lord *and my God!*"

In Acts 7:59-60, we hear the Scripture speak of the fact that when the Lord's servant Stephen was dying, "As they stoned him, Stephen prayed, "Lord Jesus, receive my spirit." He fell to his knees, shouting, "Lord, don't charge them with this sin!" And with that, he died." Last, speaking to those called to teach and serve as Overseers over God's people, the writer in Acts 20:28, says, "Guard yourselves and God's people. Feed and shepherd *God's flock—his church, purchased with his* (Jesus) *own blood—* over which the Holy Spirit has appointed you as leaders." The writer in Acts is clear, saying God the Son (Jesus) purchased the church by shedding his blood, which he did on a cross at Calvary.

CHAPTER NINE
A Love like No Other

> "BUT GOD SHOWED HIS GREAT LOVE FOR US BY SENDING CHRIST TO DIE FOR US WHILE WE WERE STILL SINNERS. AND SINCE WE HAVE BEEN MADE RIGHT IN GOD'S SIGHT BY THE BLOOD OF CHRIST, HE WILL CERTAINLY SAVE US FROM GOD'S CONDEMNATION" ROMANS 5:8-9.

From scripture, we learn and understand sin separates us from God. God not only hates sin, but he cannot look upon it, nor can it remain in his presence. The scriptures tell us the penalty deserved for sin is death, but the gift of God is eternal life. The price and punishment for sin has always been death since the beginning of humanity. Sin entered the world by the man and woman God created perfect, but they willfully disobeyed, rebelled, and transgressed against God's direct instructions. According to Genesis 2:15-17:

> "The LORD God placed the man in the Garden of Eden to tend and watch over it. But the LORD God warned him, "You may freely eat the fruit of every tree in the garden— except the tree of the knowledge of good and evil. If you eat its fruit, you are sure to die."

The man was created perfect, formed from the earth's dust by the hand of God. In his original state, he would not die, want or toil. His only task was to watch over the garden God had given him as home. However, scriptures tell us God gave the man a wife as a help-meet, and she was deceived and tricked into disobeying God, pulling her husband along in her disobedience. The scriptures read in Genesis 3:1-6:

> "The serpent was the shrewdest of all the wild animals the LORD God had made. One day he asked the woman, "Did God really say you must not eat the fruit from any of the trees in the garden?" "Of course we may eat fruit from the trees in the garden," the woman replied. "It's only the fruit from the tree in the middle of the garden that we are not allowed to eat. God said, 'You must not eat it or even touch it; if you do, you will die." "You won't die!" the serpent replied to the woman. "God knows that your eyes will be opened as soon as you eat it, and you will be like God, knowing both good and evil." The woman was convinced. She saw that the tree was beautiful, and its fruit looked delicious, and she wanted the wisdom it would give her. So she took some fruit and ate it. Then she gave some to her husband, who was with her, and he ate it, too. At that moment, their eyes were opened, and they suddenly felt shame at their nakedness."

At that very moment, the man and woman created perfectly had become fallen and imperfect. Together they committed humanity's first act of defiance and rebellion against God. As a result, he drove them from their garden paradise. They lost the perfect fellowship enjoyed with God. In its place, they received the penalty for their sin, spiritual death, physical decay, and immediate separation from the Creator that communed with them in the day's breeze in the garden. Also, they became cursed with limited days on the earth. Adam and Eve's willful act of sin condemned humanity to the penalty of sin, death, and the propensity to defy their Maker and Creator. The man's and woman's defiance originated the curse of a contentious and rebellious nature against the Divine. All men and women sin consciously and unconsciously. From birth, the predisposition to sin is part of their character. No child needs to be taught to lie or defy authority. They will do whatever necessary to avoid being punished for disobeying the command of their parents. No child needs to be taught to covet or be jealous of another over a toy, object, or item of desire or admiration. It is a natural part of their fallen nature.

We have all sinned and will continue to sin. No matter how good we attempt to be, we consistently fall beneath God's standard and expectation as his jewels among creation. The scriptures tell us in Romans 3: 23, "Everyone has sinned; we all fall short of God's glorious standard." God demands we be perfect. He insists we be as he is in thought, actions, attitude, and character. He demands and expects us to be righteous in all we do. Jesus says to us in Matthew 5: 43-48:

> "You have heard the law that says, 'Love your neighbor and hate your enemy. But I say, love your enemies! Pray for those who persecute you! In that way, you will be acting as true children of your Father in heaven. He gives his sunlight to both the evil and the good, and he sends rain on the just and the unjust alike. If you love only those who love you, what reward is there for that? If you are kind only to your friends, how are you different from anyone else? Even pagans do that. But you are to be perfect, even as your Father in heaven is perfect."

God expects us to emulate him in every way, demanding that we love our neighbors, those in our community, and not just our friends. He requires us to show kindness, even to our enemies. He wants us to love without bias, prejudice, or discrimination. Our love toward others must be unconditional, and not for the sake of personal gain or interest. He expects we be perfect as he is. Failure willfully or unintentionally is a sin and warrants his punishment.

Sin

Sin is the deliberate, intentional, and unintentional failure to meet God's standard and expectation. As humans, we sin perpetually by commission and omission. The sin of commission is the sin we commit, whether in thought, word, or deed. This sin can be intentional or unintentional. The sin of omission is sin committed because of us knowingly and deliberately failing to act or do something good or benefit someone else. We make a choice and refuse to act. The first sin of humanity committed by Adam and Eve was the sin of commission. Together, they made the deliberate choice to work in disobedience and rebellion against God. The result of their deliberate act was the penalty of death, separation, and loss of intimacy with their Creator.

In the sight of God, all sin, deliberate or unintentional, is the same. There is no such thing as a minor sin. Sin is sin. In the sight of a holy and perfect God, all sin deserves the same penalty. The penalty for sin has always been death. Since the beginning, God demanded a sacrifice for sin, and the offering was put to death in place of the offender. If no sacrifice was made or offered for sin, the offender's life is required. All men and women must pay for their sins unless they have an acceptable sacrifice to take their place. God hates sin. He will not wink or overlook evil, big or small. There is a penalty that must be paid for sin. The scriptures paint the seriousness of corruption in the sight of God by providing the

The Unchanging Truth

vivid and gruesome scene of the sacrifice demanded to atone for sin's penalty among God's people. We read in Leviticus chapter 4:

> "Then the Lord said to Moses, "Give the following instructions to the people of Israel. This is how you are to deal with those who sin unintentionally by doing anything that violates one of the Lord's commands. "If the high priest sins, bringing guilt upon the entire community, he must give a sin offering for the sin he has committed. He must present to the Lord a young bull with no defects. He must bring the bull to the Lord at the entrance of the Tabernacle, lay his hand on the bull's head, and slaughter it before the Lord. The high priest will then take some bull's blood into the Tabernacle, dip his finger in the blood, and sprinkle it seven times before the Lord in front of the inner curtain of the sanctuary. The priest will then put some blood on the altar's horns for fragrant incense that stands in the Lord's presence inside the Tabernacle. He will pour out the rest of the bull's blood at the base of the altar for burnt offerings at the entrance of the Tabernacle. Then the priest must remove all the fat of the bull to be offered as a sin offering. This includes all the fat around the internal organs, the two kidneys and the surrounding fat near the loins, and the long lobe of the liver. He must remove these along with the kidneys, just as he does with cattle offered as a peace offering, and burn them on the altar of burnt offerings. But he must take whatever is left of the bull—its hide, meat, head, legs, internal organs, and dung— and carry it away to a place outside the camp that is ceremonially clean, the place where the ashes are dumped. There, on the ash heap, he will burn it on a wood fire."
>
> "If the entire Israelite community sins by violating one of the Lord's commands, but the people don't realize it, they

are still guilty. When they become aware of their sin, the people must bring a young bull as an offering for their sin and present it before the Tabernacle. The community elders must then lay their hands on the bull's head and slaughter it before the Lord... Through this process, the priest will purify the people, making them right with the Lord, and they will be forgiven."

"If one of Israel's leaders sins by violating one of the commands of the Lord his God but doesn't realize it, he is still guilty. When he becomes aware of his sin, he must bring as his offering a male goat with no defects. He must lay his hand on the goat's head and slaughter it at the place where burnt offerings are slaughtered before the Lord. This is an offering for his sin… Through this process, the priest will purify the leader from his sin, making him right with the Lord, and he will be forgiven."

"If any of the common people sin by violating one of the Lord's commands, but they don't realize it, they are still guilty. When they become aware of their sin, they must bring as an offering for their sin a female goat with no defects. They must lay a hand on the head of the sin offering and slaughter it at the place where burnt offerings are slaughtered…Through this process, the priest will purify the people, making them right with the Lord, and they will be forgiven."

All men and women sin, sometimes deliberately and willfully, at other times unintentionally. Yet, all sin demands judgment and punishment. The sentence for corruption is death unless there is an acceptable sacrifice, perfect, and spotless. No man or woman can ever meet God's demand and expectation of perfection, nor can they serve as the spotless sacrifice. The whole of humanity is stained with the curse of sin, the byproduct of their predecessors,

Adam and Eve. However, God has provided a sacrifice. No man or woman has to stand before the righteous God and attempt to answer and justify their sins, deliberate or unintentional, sins of commission or omission. God has provided an accessible sacrifice, far more capable than bulls and goats in their place. He has offered humanity the opportunity to avoid judgment, indictment, and suffering through Christ Jesus, the Lamb of God. Whoever believes in him, as the scriptures have said, will be saved!

From the beginning, God has loved humanity, desiring intimate fellowship and relationship. At the moment Adam cursed humanity, staining us with sin, God chose to provide Jesus the second Adam to free us from sin's penalty, breaking the curse by becoming the perfect sacrifice on God's altar for sin once and for all. Because of his matchless love, God gave us his Son Jesus as the sacrifice for our sins. In John 3:16-17, we read,

> "For this is how God loved the world: He gave his one and only Son so that everyone who believes in him will not perish but have eternal life. God sent his Son into the world not to judge the world but to save the world through him."

God loved humanity so much that he withheld nothing for our redemption. Demanding the perfect sacrifice to restore humankind to an ideal relationship with himself, God provided a matchless gift. He offered the sacrifice of the highest price that could do what no other could. Jesus was delivered as a ransom by the Father to be the perfect sacrifice in our place. Only through the gift of the Lord's Christ can we be forgiven. Showing his love, God sacrificed his beloved Son to pay the penalty for sins he did not commit. Willingly, he sacrificed himself for our freedom and salvation. The writer informs us in Hebrews 10:10:

"The old system under the law of Moses was only a shadow, a dim preview of the good things to come, not the good things themselves. The sacrifices under that system were repeated again and again, year after year, but they were never able to provide perfect cleansing for those who came to worship. If they could have provided perfect cleansing, the sacrifices would have stopped, for the worshipers would have been purified once for all time, and their feelings of guilt would have disappeared." But instead, those sacrifices reminded them of their sins year after year. For it is not possible for the blood of bulls and goats to take away sins. That is why, when Christ came into the world, he said to God, "You did not want animal sacrifices or sin offerings. But you have given me a body to offer. You were not pleased with burnt offerings or other offerings for sin. Then I said,

'Look, I have come to do your will, O God—as is written about me in the Scriptures."

First, Christ said, "You did not want animal sacrifices or sin offerings or burnt offerings or other offerings for sin, nor were you pleased with them" (though the law requires them of Moses). Then he said, "Look, I have come to do your will." He cancels the first covenant to put the second into effect. For God's will was for us to be made holy by the sacrifice of the body of Jesus Christ, once for all time."

CHAPTER TEN
Hell is a Real Place

"IF YOUR HAND CAUSES YOU TO STUMBLE, CUT IT OFF. IT IS BETTER FOR YOU TO ENTER LIFE MAIMED THAN WITH TWO HANDS TO GO INTO HELL, WHERE THE FIRE NEVER GOES OUT" MARK 9:43.

HELL IS AN actual place! Although difficult for most to imagine, there is a place where lost men and women will spend eternity separated from the presence, light, and love of God. There is a place where the disobedient and Christ-rejecting, those that die in their sins, will spend eternity in darkness, terror, and never quenching desperation and regret. This place, created and reserved for the fallen angels, has enlarged itself because of humanity's willful and often deliberate sin. The words of the Lord Jesus are recorded in Matthew 13:40-43:

> "Just as the weeds are sorted out and burned in the fire, so it will be at the end of the world. The Son of Man will send his angels, and they will remove from his Kingdom everything that causes sin and all who do evil. And the angels will throw them into the fiery furnace, where there will be weeping and gnashing of teeth. Then the righteous

will shine like the sun in their Father's Kingdom. Anyone with ears to hear should listen and understand!"

Many deceive themselves in believing such a place is the creation and fiction of imaginations. However, that is not the case. The concept of the afterlife has survived in practically every civilization that has ever existed. Humanity has long understood that man's soul, the life force, is far too powerful to cease to exist, and continues in some form in the beyond. Many civilizations and societies have long subscribed and accepted that multiple options existed for the soul to spend eternity, either a destination of peace and pleasure, or a place of sadness, torment, and never ending eternal destruction. Even the ancient Egyptians believed life does not end after we transition from this plane. They believed the last judgment took place before their god Osiris, the god of the dead. They believed the heart was weighed and balanced against the feather of truth. If the scales balanced, the god Osiris would permit the deceased into the paradise called the Field of Reeds. In contrast, if the scales failed to balance because of the hearts heaviness with sin, the monster Ammit, described as having a Crocodile head and called the Eater and Devourer of the Dead, will destroy and render them to an eternity of shame and torment.

Many resist the idea that hell or a place of punishment exists. However, Jesus declared there is such a place. In the book of Luke, Jesus does not offer a parable as he often did to his listeners. He shared a story that included figures, people, and well known characters. The scripture reads in Luke 16:19-30:

> "Jesus said, "There was a certain rich man who was splendidly clothed in purple and fine linen and who lived each day in luxury. At his gate lay a poor man named Lazarus, who was covered with sores. As Lazarus lay there longing for scraps from the rich man's table, the dogs would come

and lick his open sores. "Finally, the poor man died and was carried by the angels to be with Abraham. The rich man also died and was buried, and his soul went to the place of the dead. There, in torment, he saw Abraham in the far distance with Lazarus at his side. "The rich man shouted, 'Father Abraham, have some pity! Send Lazarus over here to dip the tip of his finger in water and cool my tongue. I am in anguish in these flames. "But Abraham said to him, 'Son, remember that during your lifetime you had everything you wanted, and Lazarus had nothing. So now he is here being comforted, and you are in anguish. And besides, there is a great chasm separating us. No one can cross over to you from here, and no one can cross over to us from there.' "Then the rich man said, 'Please, Father Abraham, at least send him to my father's home. I have five brothers, and I want him to warn them, so they don't end up in this place of torment.' "But Abraham said, 'Moses and the prophets have warned them. Your brothers can read what they wrote.' "The rich man replied, 'No, Father Abraham! But if someone is sent to them from the dead, then they will repent of their sins and turn to God.'"

From this passage, we conclude that Jesus attempts to convince his audience of their need to repent, turn from sin, and avoid an impending judgment and punishment. Jesus does not use unknown characters; he is specific, saying the rich man pleaded with the father of the faithful "Abraham" and was reminded of the pleasures and comforts he enjoyed in life and his neglect of the poor. But now, in the place of the dead where wealth, position, and title have no value or worth, God remembers the poor. Here for all eternity, the poor man will be comforted while the rich, arrogant, and those that found hope and comfort in wealth and attainments, rejecting God and His Christ suffer never-ending torment and agony.

When life is over, all men and women will spend eternity either in the loving, tender, and gentle embrace of fellowship with the God of Creation and their Savior Christ Jesus or in outer darkness, the place of anguish, torment, and pain. Regarding The Final Judgment, the writer tells us in Matthew 25:31-46:

> "When the Son of Man comes in his glory and all the angels with him, then he will sit upon his glorious throne. All the nations will be gathered in his presence, and he will separate the people as a shepherd separates the sheep from the goats. He will place the sheep at his right hand and the goats at his left. "Then the King will say to those on his right, 'Come, you who are blessed by my Father, inherit the Kingdom prepared for you from the creation of the world. I was hungry, and you fed me. I was thirsty, and you gave me a drink. I was a stranger, and you invited me into your home. I was naked, and you gave me clothing. I was sick, and you cared for me. I was in prison, and you visited me.' "Then these righteous ones will reply, 'Lord, when did we ever see you hungry and feed you? Or thirsty and give you something to drink? Or a stranger and show you hospitality? Or naked and give you clothing? When did we ever see you sick or in prison and visit you?' "And the King will say, 'I tell you the truth when you did it to one of the least of these my brothers and sisters, you were doing it to me!' "Then the King will turn to those on the left and say, 'Away with you, you cursed ones, into the eternal fire prepared for the devil and his demons. I was hungry, and you didn't feed me. I was thirsty, and you didn't give me a drink. I was a stranger, and you didn't invite me into your home. I was naked, and you didn't

give me clothing. I was sick and in prison, and you didn't visit me.' "Then they will reply, 'Lord, when did we ever see you hungry or thirsty or a stranger or naked or sick or in prison, and not help you?' "And he will answer, 'I tell you the truth when you refused to help the least of these my brothers and sisters, you were refusing to help me.' "And they will go away into eternal punishment, but the righteous will go into eternal life."

Many deny rigorously the reality of Hell. However, the Scripture has much to say affirming its existence. Not as a metaphor, but as a physical and tangible place. Suggesting what we might consider extreme, the writer in Mark 9:42-48 records the words of the Lord Jesus saying,

"If you cause one of these little ones who trust in me to fall into sin, it would be better for you to be thrown into the sea with a large millstone hung around your neck. If your hand causes you to sin, cut it off. It's better to enter eternal life with only one hand than to go into the unquenchable fires of hell with two hands. If your foot causes you to sin, cut it off. It's better to enter eternal life with only one foot than to be thrown into hell with two feet. And if your eye causes you to sin, gouge it out. It's better to enter the Kingdom of God with only one eye than to have two eyes and be thrown into hell, 'where the maggots never die, and the fire never goes out.'"

If we did not have the scriptures as a record, other secondary sources would confirm the historical existence of the Jewish Rabbi Saul of Tarsus. Historical records corroborate he lived, traveled, evangelized, was imprisoned, and died a martyr in Rome for his witness of Jesus, the LORD's Christ. The apostle Paul, highly educated, well trained, intellectual, and a superb apologist, offered an encouragement to believers and followers of Christ Jesus in the city of Thessalonica, saying according to 2 Thessalonians 1:5-10:

> "God will use this persecution to show his justice and to make you worthy of his Kingdom, for which you are suffering. In his justice, he will pay back those who persecute you. And God will provide rest for you who are being persecuted and for us when the Lord Jesus appears from heaven. He will come with his mighty angels, in flaming fire, bringing judgment on those who don't know God and on those who refuse to obey the Good News of our Lord Jesus. They will be punished with eternal destruction, forever separated from the Lord and from his glorious power. When he comes on that day, he will receive glory from his holy people—praise from all who believe. And this includes you, for you believed what we told you about him."

Willful and unrepentant sin will be punished. However, it is more appropriate to assert that no sin will go unpunished. The penalty for sin is death. God views all sin the same. In Jude's book, it gives an example of sexual immorality using Sodom and Gomorrah's cities, pointing out that the inhabitants desired, practice, and perform unnatural sexual acts, besides the mistreatment of strangers. For these wicked and sinful acts, they received the punishment of fire falling from heaven, consuming and destroying them. The punishment of fire and eternal destruction is the judgment for all sin not atoned for by Christ's precious blood shed on the cross. The writer said in Jude 1:7:

> "Don't forget Sodom and Gomorrah and their neighboring towns, which were filled with immorality and every kind of sexual perversion. Those cities were destroyed by

fire and serve as a warning of the eternal fire of God's judgment."

Hell is an actual place, reserved for the arrogant, proud, and disobedient. The deceived will be lost, without hope, and condemned to suffer an avoidable judgment. Doubting men and women can choose Christ, the accepted propitiation for the sins of the entire world. God is not a Santa Claus, nor is his Christ, the little babe in the manger. He is the Savior of the world. Christ is the Suffering Servant who came to save the lost, hopeless, and dying from the penalty of sin. However, many reject him, believing Hell does not exist, and that there will be no reckoning for their defiance and sin filled lives. In their delusion they rationalize God would not create such a place nor send them there. However, God does not send or condemn; men and women ignorantly choose to worship the creature in place of the Creator, condemning themselves. The writer warns against such ignorance saying in Revelations 14:9-11:

> "Anyone who worships the beast and his statue or who accepts his mark on the forehead or on the hand must drink the wine of God's anger. It has been poured full strength into God's cup of wrath. And they will be tormented with fire and burning sulfur in the presence of the holy angels and the Lamb. The smoke of their torment will rise forever and ever, and they will have no relief day or night, for they have worshiped the beast and his statue and have accepted the mark of his name."

Last, speaking of the Final Judgment of Humanity, when the books are opened, and the names of men and women are read, the writer John says in Revelation 20:10:

> "Then death and the grave were thrown into the lake of fire. This lake of fire is the second death. And anyone whose name was not found recorded in the Book of Life was thrown into the lake of fire."

Hell is a real place, and the punishment awaiting the unbelieving is unimaginable and without end. However, no one has to experience the judgment and penalty for sin. Christ Jesus came into the world to save the lost. He has already paid the price for sin. Men and women need only to believe in him (Jesus), as the scriptures have said, and they will be saved from the wrath of God that is to come. If Hell is not real, there would have been no need for Jesus to come into the world he created and die on a tree like a common criminal, though he was innocent, faultless, and claimless. However, because he loved us, he died in our place. We are reminded in John 3:16, "For this is how God loved the world: He gave his one and only Son so that everyone who believes in him will not perish but have eternal life."

The judgment of God will someday come, and humanity will receive what they deserve. Speaking of that day, the writer records in Zephaniah 1:14-18:

> "That terrible day of the LORD is near. Swiftly it comes—a day of bitter tears, a day when even strong men will cry out. It will be a day when the LORD's anger is poured out— a day of terrible distress and anguish, a day of ruin and desolation, a day of darkness and gloom, a day of clouds and blackness, a day of trumpet calls and battle cries. Down go the walled cities and the strongest battlements! "Because you have sinned against the Lord, I will make you grope around like the blind. Your blood will be poured into the dust, and your bodies will lie rotting on the ground." Your silver and gold will not save you on that

day of the Lord's anger. The whole land will be devoured by the fire of his jealousy. He will make a terrifying end of all the people on earth."

Final Thoughts

At the writing of this book, the world is in the grips of one of the most challenging plagues to ever confront humanity, COVID-19. In the United States alone 16,549,366 cases have been reported, and 305,082 deaths. The world as we have known it in the past will never be the same. Nothing will ever be as it was. As a society and world, we must anticipate, create, and accept change as a new normal. The end of this worldwide pandemic is nowhere in sight. We are all in this challenge and struggle together.

Though blame has been cast without substantiation, no one has a clear and definite answer for the origin of this relentless virus. No one knows where it actually came from or when it will make its exit. For the first time in millennia, humanity is faced with an irrefutable reality, we are not in control. There is something at work, greater, stronger, and with an unwavering purpose. Perhaps men and women should consider the possibility that the origin of this so-called Corona virus is God, the creator of heaven and earth. Speaking of God's anger toward his creation, the writer in the book of Isaiah said in Isaiah 24:4-6:

> "The earth mourns and dries up, and the land wastes away and withers. Even the greatest people on earth waste away. The earth suffers for the sins of its people, for they have

twisted God's instructions, violated his laws, and broken his everlasting covenant. Therefore, a curse consumes the earth. Its people must pay the price for their sin."

Speaking to his disciples about what to anticipate at the closing, conclusion, and ending of this present age Jesus affirmed in Luke 21:11,

"Nation will go to war against nation, and kingdom against kingdom. There will be great earthquakes, and there will be famines and plagues in many lands, and there will be terrifying things and great miraculous signs from heaven."

God is in control of every aspect of our world. Nothing escapes him. He never sleeps nor does he slumber. In the midst of his own calamity Job said in Job 12:7-10:

"Just ask the animals, and they will teach you. Ask the birds of the sky, and they will tell you. Speak to the earth, and it will instruct you. Let the fish in the sea speak to you. For they all know that my disaster has come from the hand of the LORD. For the life of every living thing is in his hand, and the breath of every human being."

He is in control and he does care. He loves us more than words can express. It is his great joy that his beloved children come and turn to him. He desires nothing more than to heal, rescue, and save. No matter where we are, what we have found ourselves in, or the circumstance that seems unbearable, we can call on God. No matter how bad we have messed up. No matter how disobedient we have been. No matter how defiant and rebellious we have chosen to be. He is there and willing to help us, if we repent, turning from our waywardness, and have a change of heart and mind. He has assured us that he will save us if we cry out to him earnestly and sincerely, acknowledging him as our only hope. Speaking to Solomon after the dedication of the Holy Temple in Jerusalem, God says in 2 Chronicles 7:13-14:

> "At times I might shut up the heavens so that no rain falls, or command grasshoppers to devour your crops, or send plagues among you. Then if my people who are called by my name will humble themselves and pray and seek my face and turn from their wicked ways, I will hear from heaven and will forgive their sins and restore their land."

www.ingramcontent.com/pod-product-compliance
Lightning Source LLC
Chambersburg PA
CBHW022123040426
42450CB00006B/820